# Before There Were Guns, There Were Gods

To: Cenise ♡

Thank you for your love's & support!! You are a beautiful light, keep shining brightly my love!.

Love

Ayenna McNeil

# Before There Were Guns, There Were Gods

Ayanna M. McNeill

**To order additional copies of this book, contact:**
Xlibris Corporation
1-888-795-4274
www.Xlibris.com
Orders@Xlibris.com
74216

# CONTENTS

Dedicated to Amadou, you are the light at the end of my tunnel and I shine because I am filled with love for you. I love and miss you brother.

# The Bullet and The Ballot

Guns blazing through city streets
Utica Ave. is like a battle field
Nine year olds pulling triggers

Spreading bullets like semen over da'
Hood
Open wounds point the blame at hot steel
Thousands die, as NRA boost
Second amendment rights to destruction

# Fulton Street Revolution

## *My first African Street Festival Experience*

Substance leaks from my pores as I bask in sunlight
I suck up the smells of Caribbean and Puerto Rican cuisines
And apple fritters
I hear children rejoicing over inflatable toys and the ice cream truck
In the distance I hear African sistahs bargaining a painting
And then there were the drums
They summoned me to center stage and penetrated my spirit
To spit fire at the anxious crowd
Who shouted like it was
Sunday morning when I asked
"Why the hell are there more baby daddies than libraries in our communities?"
or "How come that crack game is still being played?"
are we being played?
      I felt forty-one spontaneous pains when Timothy was shot through
his crown
                  DAMN what a sight!
He fell just like Amadou Diallo fell down
Without dignity and justice for all
As his RED blood penetrated the WHITE project cement under the misty
BLUE skies
Signifying all that Amerikkka stands for
      BOO-A-KA BOO-A-KA
What about the raise in milk prices that floods our homes and makes it hard
For our WIC checks to stay afloat
4—something a gallon
should be measured as a pain in the ass

yet we are still 'all good with living in the hood'
yes gentle people;
      "What would Fulton Street be without . . ."
beggers,
bodegas,
liquor,
low life hookers,
stores called Associate,
crime advocates,
politics hiding behind church crosses
or Mr. Chin cooking chicken better than we can
      Yes what would Black Amerikkka be without it's
Tims,
Rims,
Slick-backs,
Or a fat ass,
Super sized ignorance from the drive thru view,
Or like Lauyrn Hill prophesized fake hair from Europeans and nails done
by Koreans

AND THE DRUMS CONTINUE
      Boo-a-ka Boo-a-ka
Bed-Stuy Do or Die
Rang out as I was pushed up next in line
Handed a pen
And told to begin
The REVOLUTION

# My Testament

I feel like a newborn sinner
Placed again in a world to be a destruction to myself
forced to fight demons with bare hands and tarnished determination
struggling to breathe hearing church sisters behind me
humming and taunting me
my body rocks like slave ships anchored to colonial religions
like Easter day and Christmas giving
my eyes water and salt runs down my cheek
still being crucified for being born a queen
crown knocked down by my own people with no-lye relaxers
Ain't like niggers done got too relaxed
they are busy painting artificial artifacts
of sacrilegious rap images on store fronts and train stops
Jesus with a pipe in his arm on 1 2 fifth
Do not throw stones at my tongue because I choose to admit
Brothers rather die for momentary highs
while sisters will get down on their knees
to suck corruption from Lucifer's loins
I feel like a newborn sinner
Walking on Air
we are Force Ones
pushed into a culture where the Bible must be paraphrased in sake of the gun
Hell-like fires blazing burned up desires in ghetto housing with wired up
cable and disabled beliefs
decapitated geniuses with long slung penises
producing the anti-Christ on vinyl and c.d.'s
my feet baptized in murky waters as I walk over baffled niggers
Angels named Corretta, Malcolm, and Huey walk swiftly beside me
Saying, take a breath and believe
That God builds bridges and God burns bridges, just to get you to the
other side
So, cross one wilderness into another threshold
I once felt like a sinner reborn
But then I met poetry and I was saved.

# Beauty Queen's Poem

When I was twelve I nursed a baby with my bare breast
And I worked a 9 until on the streets with no rest
As chrome wheels made my stomach
toss and turn
could this be another sale?
I twist my hips, raise my skirt, lower my shirt and lick my lips
As my clit starts to swell
As much as I hate sexing old dirty men
                    I am still a woman, aren't I?


When I was 15
Abortions became a regular thing
My daddy told me to do things like my mommy use to . . .
And I did
But that don't mean I got to have his babies
1 then 2
3 more
all gone for
two hundred and fifteen dollars and now my stomach is sore
my breast hang
from the baby milk
that I drink when mama
spends the grocery money on heroin
She's zoned out
She just leans to the side
With a needle in her neck
And no feelings
                    So daddy feels on me


When I was 22
My hands slid down
Cold steel poles
To feed the bad asses that I had at home
No other man is gonna take care of me and my father's kids

So I get paid by
Shaking ass, dropping ass, stripping ass and giving head
Platinum chains make my heart beat fast
Maybe I can get my light turned on and stop selling ass
But these men are all the same
Cheap, broken and in the game

Tomorrow got to go to the clinic

Today got to pray
Two weeks pass and I've got AIDS

Two years pass and I am still on stage
*Shaking ass, dropping ass, stripping ass, and giving head*
I can't even count how many men I did
Hope their families have life *in. sure. ance*
How do you spell that anyways?
I didn't go to school since

When I was 12 I breastfeed
And got my cherry popped by old dirty men in chrome wheels
And by 15
Abortions became a regular thing
And at 22 my hands slid down
Cold steel poles
Now I am 26
Cold dead and still alone

# Revo/lized Rhymes . . .
# on and on and it don't stop . . . .

Knee knockin head boppin' beats
Got me harmonizing
Screaming I WAS GETTING SOME HEAD
Instead of moving ahead
I am prolonging the revol/motion
With dia-dia-diamonds on my neck
No hands to direct change in Sierra Leone`
I been gone, too far gone
Rocking emeralds in spiral gold dust
Hanging off cliff rocks
And I am rolling
Rollin down the river
Forever hustling
pushing it to the limit
Brothers dying before 22
Can't even graduate from High School at 22
But real quick to talk about fucking in room 222
Never-ending traditions . . . we been rhyming
Been spitting and emceeing and field tripping
Knee deep in cotton . . . . Just call us The Jumpman
Because we been leaping over Jordan(s)
Chasing freedom
We been singing . . . revo/motion
Grinding like clockwork
Whistling spirituals while we worked

No chains . . . now we are conceited
What's the reason?
Call it culture
Or call it assimilation
White collar vultures
Sign checks and resurrect mental slavery
Picking those ins
Trying to get by, profits gotta stay high I-I-I-I
Or we were bound to die
We made beats out of tree trunks
And turned centuries over tables
And it don't stop and it don't stop and it don't stop
Uh don't push or we'll shove back
No more chanting in sit-ins
We think we fit it
Can't buy freedom with 50CENT
Just rocked out with bling bling
No longer slingin' our way through warfare
Shit ain't fair
Booty bouncing
Whips on my neck and my back
Pussy poppin on the handstand
Exploitation in rap land
No long a revolution
We been revo/lized

# They Used to Kill Poets

## 03.25.04

*Dedicated to the Runaway slaves of the 21ˢᵗ Century and BBACD*

As revealed in Revelations 3:22
     **"He that hath an ear, let him hear what the Spirit saith unto the churches"**
I, the spirit scream
"They Used To Kill Poets"
for we were not convinced life was about open orgasms and idle time to spare
us love revolutionaries were so provocative, we were feared
we were the voices of God that led Moses
we birth salvation in the Congo and burned with four little angels in churches
we were the strange fruits
dripping bloody juices into Amerikkka's roots
and the infant cries of South Africa
who knew Apartheid aided AIDS
James Byrd Jr. left a trail of poetic verses as
He was dragged through the city of *Sodom* and *Gomorrah*
     We filled open mics with the power of lighting and thunder
Abner Louima rolled with the Roots and Emmett Till
We were the hands that allowed the world to feel
And we sat next to Mandela and Martin in jail
"They Used To Kill Poets"
for standing eloquently in courthouses

To fight for sitting in the front                          of the struggle
Like brother Jamar said *"we are still a product in the White Man's hustle"*
he betta watch his sanity
because
"They Used To Kill Poets"
        don't you know it?
we got sistah Cook *"telling brothas if the shoe fits, wear it to walk with her while honoring the old heads"*
and Mama Wright-Lewis tells all her kids
*"a nigger I am not, a nigger I will never be, I am not afraid of freedom or prosperity"*
"They Used To Kill Poets"
like black men with books
like Nakita and Jelani
        they shot them off project roof tops for being kings
they strangled and raped queens like Ms. Samuels or Sharisse, or Nikki the original G
for they envied their abilities
"They Used To Kill Poets"
as predominate as Harriet Tubman, Sister Maisha, and Sadiquah
who lead the blind to see
                        ***Freedom***
        Through love
I can't forget that some still try to crucify me
Cuz when slaves could not read
I was in love with poetry

# He Finally got the Y

I remember it like the scar on my knee
The day Ms. Emma's body found her beat
With the cuticles of her fingers dyed blood red
As her son laid dying in the softness of her silk suit
Gun shots that rang out after the school bell rang
Sent Emma's blossoming seed reversing the
"Circle of Life" as he carried a "Lion King" folder
And Emma's body trembles as her tears overcame her
She releases an inhumane shout
How could she have been late that day,
When bullets whizzed by third graders
And landed in her son's chest?
Blood drips as if it were trying to emulate the Nile's flow
Masked cowards run in place with nowhere to go
They can't hide from their neighbors
Who use to lend them cereal
Who know the serial numbers of their guns.
I remember it like cotton candy melting on the tip of my tongue
The way she physically felt the physical rocking of the slave ships

She rocked like how grandma use to rock in the church aisles
Wearing pastels
At Easter Sunday
She reminisces about buying her son a sundae
Now her sun has gone down
Down into the depths of the concrete's crack
She huddles over her son's fallen chest
Pain creeping up her back
She throws her hands to the sky
Searching through the misty air
For answers why
Why, why, why???
Y was the letter her first grader had a hard time with
But he was finally coming to grips
Spelling H-A-P-P-Y
As the bullets ripped
Through his sweet limitless heart
I remember it like rain against the Mississippi Magnolia trees
The day Ms. Emma's body danced for me

# Forget Not: Sankofa

*To The African Burial Ground Ceremony*

Destitute, stripped, and confused
Cultural holocaust, ancient kings and queens abused
      But Sankofa reminds us
Covered with concrete and capitalism
Silenced by whips, that's why we could not hear them
      The wind serenades Sankofa
Through the malice and the mayhem
They've survived through the strife
1645 was the year we were exempt from serfdom and expected to serve life
life lower than cattle
and now we wonder why the cows are mad
      the drums scream Sankofa
It's LITERAL
Buildings sit on top of your remains
Your bones hold up their shaky frames
      The pressure of the steel squeaks Sankofa
Reburial in respect of your greatness
But your contributions still have not been recognized in this nation
So as a substitute you pulled down the twins
      Yelling out REPARATIONS
      Handclaps praise Sankofa
My hand shakes as the black runs out of my pen
But my eyes water because our State Pens never run out of blacks
And my temples throb as I try to explain to our ancestors
Why Kareem is on the corner selling his dignity
Instead of being royalty
      Rock capsules hit the ground and cry Sankofa
Young girls perm their hair because they fear kinkiness
The same kinks that make sure their crowns don't slip
      Combs break the mold and whisper Sankofa
But through it all
      Sankofa breathes
      Sankofa Lives
As you are laid to rest
      Sankofa Continues

# The Shape of an Afr—I—Can

Sitting on stolen property
Countries become pieces of monopoly
Little white girls conditioning niggers to see purity
Sitting at cherry wood pianos tickling keys of ivory
Blood trickling on the cords from colonialism and slavery
Afr—I—Can hands are the black keys
The dark pieces missing in the puzzle
Our backs against enslavement and our faces up against a gun nozzle
Afr—I—Can; I think I can; I say therefore I am
Condemn to see paintings of whiteys and pianos
And my soul knows
That we are sitting on stolen property
Conditioning throughout history
As children of thievery
Finders keepers, losers weepers
Got older and the plot got deeper
They teach that America is everyone's land
They teach that Africa belongs to all because it's the birthplace of all man
But Europe is just for Europeans
And Japanese are in complete control of Japan
Where is African-American land?
We are sitting on stolen property?
Where is our milk and honey?
Our sun blazed hills of golden stanzas
Little white 'Janes' make Africans look like monkeys on a chase for bananas
Where are our temples and our national flag?
We've been forced to lift every voice and sing
Screaming "Let Freedom Ring"
But all I hear is the soft stroke of their fingers
Dried up blood under their nails and hatred in their songs
Diamonds on their fingers from Sierra Leon`
Little white girls saying "I can't"
But I hold my head high and remember my name
I always was and will be an AFR—I—CAN

# Ashy

I laughed today until my soul was full with content and my eyes watered with joy
I forgot that I had blood stains on my shirt and that my cheeks were ashy from tears
I laughed until the media no longer pumped up my fears
Remembering
Holding my lover's hand through cold steel boundaries
He was placed in a cell              to              mate
To insure the destruction of our future
He now finds nurture
In a man's hand
Instead of my heavenly center
I laughed harder today, until my heart became tender
I rode the bus sitting next to Rosa

Perez
Who has five soldiers and a lost warrior
Her man becomes crack
Because growing up . . .
It was a daddy she lacked
          I made her laugh
Until she forgot her stretch marks and unpaid bills
I forgot the body pieces under the bus's wheels

I taught my eleven year old niece what I was able
On her roach infested table
She needs a new              guide
Because she has become      dense
She hides her insecurities by opening her legs
Pregnancy she now faces
But we laughed anyways

I laughed until spontaneous pain that use to come as regular as my monthly
                                    Bills
Now flees as my smile grows
        I walk down the street and kick a bum's beer over
        I expect him to cut me for taking his

        Sanity
So I say it was a mistake
But he just laughs foolishly and
                    So do I

I blink twice and now recognize

The blood stains
                Rosa,
                    My lost illicit lover
                                And the bum
And my cheeks become ashy

                                    Again.

# Little Alter Boys

Priests groping little alter boys that's what I see
A man's penis is just that, even with a vow of celibacy
Crack robs women of their royalties and kills our growing babies
Being trusting of a faith is so hard
When every war of RAGE is titled "I N  T H E  N A M E  O F  G O D"
I didn't have a history book so
PAKISTAN
       AND
            ISRAEL
Helped me understand the crusades
9-11 even schooled me on the patriotic way
I found out that Sierra Leone swims in blood
Egypt's lands are barren because our queen's rivers refuse to flood
        But pass the priest
I have to think about the rats on my city's streets
Four-year-olds get bitten while others trip on the new Jay-Z and Beyonce's
beats
Hip Hop was not about bling bling or that crack sling
It had a message of Marcus Garvey, Booker T, and Malcolm X that rang
Hip hop oozed with pride of being ORIGINAL
But we didn't know it though
                            Our cows are going mad because
Of the way we slaughter them
Shit, now everyone wants to be a Muslim
                 *"no pork please"*
ain't that funny?
       And
            BILLION dollar Bloomberg
                         Wants to add
Smart guns and police to protect us in school
Instead of protecting our brains they rather have
Secured FOOLS

What about the AIDS season
Where GENOCIDE is the reason
I can't see that the government hopes for the destruction of our communities
Cuz all I can focus on is how . . . HABEB is trying to terrorize me
My conscience get RAPED behind another Bush
Being a woman or a man is rushed
       12 year old fathers and mothers' wombs that haven't reached a decade
and all I can see is the queen of England's teeth decay
as she smiles DEVILISHLY knowing damn well she is mocking ME
I once was a Queen,
But now I am down with the black Diamond Revolutionaries
After I saw
       PRIEST GROPING
       LITTLE ALTER BOYS
In a VOW of CELIBACY

# Cornrows

## *Ode to Gerren Liles*

Blacks never really liked corn/rows
Or back lashing, sun beaming, and cotton barrels
      They didn't find the word nigger compassionate
How could ancient kings and queens ever accept a term like that?

In fact, our men could never grow pass the title of 'boy'
And our women were forced to fill the void of fatherhood
They became the sole provider
      That's why sistahs are now so comfortable being single mothers
Sagging pants or the newest kicks
      Were not our concern when we had fields to pick
And family was sacred and could not be captured on a television show
It was love that made the sun glow

They didn't know about mad cows' disease because the cattle had it better
than them
A book was freedom, and their tragedies could not be captured on some
Amastad film

      The enslaved mothers were the ones who emancipated the rest
They cooked, taught, and cleaned up our mess
There was so many Rosas, Assatas, or Corettas, that it was pointless
      To ever except the fact we are hoes or bitches, we were God sent

But let's not forget, a family without a father has not been blessed
It wasn't Abe Lincoln who built our liberties, it was our enslaved kings who
sweated determination under the rays of slavery

It was the granddaddies
Who schooled us on The Temptations and The Emotions
      Of voting

It's the fathers who stuck it out for you and me
And it is the brothers who desire to one day be the producers of our babies

Hip hop can return to it's original form
      Slave spirituals and the African drum
50 Cent will only be in our pockets
and education and de-gentrification is what we will market
like Alicia Keys said "we can put these armors down and settle down"
and untangle the indoctrinating styles that have been titled full of soul
we will start wearing crowns instead of            cornrows

# Georgia Thunder Storms

they say in time you will forget
but still my eyes are wet
every time it storms in Georgia

head hung low under burdens I have stored
the thunder rings unspoken melodies of pain
they say "GOD IS ANGRY"

I heard Church Bells spell hypocrisy
the wind is crisp, and it chokes me
the rain blends in with my own tears as a masquerade

puddles capture my feet
as anger raptures in my chest
tightness encloses me
and I cannot breathe

I have something on my mind
something that walks next to me
lulls me to sleeps
and awakes me again in a cold sweat

I hear it whisper through my poetry
and dance in my music
I cannot shake it
misery likes company

And I have reluctantly become its best friend
closest comrades, learning that there will be no end to my distress
I often have Georgia on my mind
every time it rains it pours
and I become sour

they said this too shall pass
the storm will clear
and the "LORD WILL BE THERE"

I hope I can hold out until Salvation comes
the sun keeps slipping away
and I am consumed with darkness
every time lightning strikes the skies

I close my eyes and pray
hoping He see it fit for me to survive
just another day . . . I hang my head and face the demons as they come
I am only one.

# America's New Anthem

Land of the whip, home of the slave
Everyday my ancestors scream from their graves
The ancient essence of my culture has begun to decay
The one who stands strong under the weight of the world, those are the brave
Like the Afrikan proverb said "Before they came, we had the land and they
had the bible and after they came we had the bible, and they had the land"
That is master plan
After the immaculate conception of our damnation
The British East Indian Company built schools for the spread of our
miseducation
And we are so quick to glorify some damn man-made lies
The same lies that forces all of our children to die
Take a quick glance at this black supremacist here to let you know
Fuck what you heard, and you can take that to CoinTellPro
Because from the mainstream non-violent protestors of Birmingham to the
by-any-means necessary followers of Malcolm
Righteousness will rise up in every ghetto and every slum
For all true citizens know
Land of the whip, Home of the slave
Everyday my ancestors scream from their graves
American's New Anthem

# Explosive

## *My First Year at Lincoln*

Explosive
Mind blowing conspiracies being thrown at me everyday
From the way Mother Earth has become a Man's World
To the way we are conditioned to forever be boys and girls
The way nigger freely slips through our black beautiful lips
And how the harshness of 'bitch' has being misplaced with compassion
YO I CALL BITCH BECAUSE I LOVE YOU BITCH
But check this
As I lick my wounds and keeping rolling
My royalties that once were not denied of me
Are now forgotten
How can I be someone's Queen
While living under the restrains of IHOP
INTERNATIONAL HOUSE OF PUSSY
Well pop this piece of intellect in your skull
And let's grow
Let's become sun children again
Since we were where it all began
Let us remember what it felt like to dip our toes in the Nile
But lets not forget the scars of hardships, and isms and oppression on our
frames
For they still remains

Fresh
Explosive
And very much relevant
So brothers lets not disregard that equals must exist to survive
If thou are king then every sistah you meet is queen
And should be treated as such
And sisters enough is enough
Disrespect is not a stranger to the self
In other words, you are what you display
No play
We be mothers and destiny is ours
So act as such
And then no one will label you as a slut
Yes
Explosive
Fresh
Mind blowing conspiracies even
I am just prophesying on what I am seeing.

# How to Take the Boyz out of the Hood and Make Men from Niggas

Step 1 is to restore your rightful strength to where it should be
To disvalue the misconceptions that power lies in bullets
Let's rebuild brains
One molecule at a time
Let's replace sugar waters
With much sweeter juices
Fruits pulled from trees of intellect
Step 2 Let's neglect the tracking devices on our hips
Let's communicate with the stars
No jobs to enslave us
Why don't we create careers
We be whatever we be
And no textbook, BET, radio, rapper, or paper
Can define us
How to take the Boys out of the hood and the Men from Niggas
Give them books to travel on
Ancient lands with ancient knowledge
Give them crowns decked out with diamonds beyond bling bling
And rubies from royal blood
Leave scriptures by their bedside
To play the role of a guide
Toward righteousness
Take the grim from the streets
And the streets from their livelihood
Rebirth their purpose
And rinse their souls
Become their baptism
Step 3 is a hassle—
Making a man himself, whole, and perfect in his imperfections
A task many times left un-tackled

Picking up the tiny pieces
And becoming like glue
        Binding
Never halting always finding
Another nigga in a man
We must use our fingertips
To scratch the surface
Baring the warrior scars
Our words must bring tears and laughter
We have to become a boisterous river washing
The enslaving views from his temples
We become sacks
Carrying some of the load
And we are the bodies of books making sure history is told
How to make men from niggaz
Revise renaissances
And replay Marvin Gaye
And Billie or Donny Hathaway
Minnie Ripperton or Duke Ellington
Our eyes must reach depth never touched
Incarnations of God, shining and healing
Take our wombs and become shooting stars
The greatest orgasm
A poignant rocking
Back and forth
Creating friction
And becoming groundbreaking
We must plant seeds in concrete
And then use Black Magic to make them grow
How to take the Boys out of the Hood and make Men from Niggas?
We create 40 days of Mass destruction and 40 nights of procreation
We become the ultimate rebirth

# The Greatest Threat

*Ode to Assata: keep roaming black cat*

WHERE MY RUNAWAY SLAVES OF THE 21<sup>st</sup> CENTURY?
*Right here*
Let me school you on this piece of history
The Greatest Threat
To the threads that sew us into a worthless stature
Where being human doesn't matter
Where lying next to your brother in a body bag is on the regular
It's like centuries old shackles that start to make your skin sag
It's the constant pounding in your chest
A bullet shot
Or two or three
WHO SHOT YA, ASSATA?
My African queen
Whose jewels have been tarnished and twisted
Yet your feet
God has kissed your feet

You've escaped
The slave masters
Who have yet to master
The magic of your magnificent departure
RUN BUTTERFLY RUN
Until our pain crusts over and festers
Shout out the fallen ones for they need to know
Salvation comes not from a gun
And don't worry I'll read to your grandbabies
I'll read so profound and poetically
I'll read as if you were me
So PURR ON black cat
Cuz one day you'll roam back
Into the psyche of those struck with un/remembrance
And then you and I shall dance
As if African soil tickles our toes again
We won't be enslaved then
Or runaway royalty of the 21<sup>st</sup> century
We'll be FREE

# When They Came Along

Black bruises on mahogany skin
Mellow moans over elevated syn/copated beats
Hands involuntarily ripped vessel and pillaged through valleys
Taking years in seconds, minutes of sweat glistens
Heartbeat racing as his penetrated paradise surrounds him
Outburst of fire, release of evil, devilish desires
Looking down at her whitened womb
Eyes closed too painfully for her to consume
Premature leaders wiped from her thighs
Hand rough, closing her teary eyes
Black bruises on mahogany skin
Hallow cavities rapidly releasing rambunctious ridicules of slavery
Where our Kings were castrated and forced to

                     **R**elive the warmth of
                     **A**frica by wrongly
                     **P**enetrating the wombs of
                     **E**ve

Black bruises on mahogany skin
Black people dropped in Babylon forced begin
Life over, after centuries of pushing watermelons and pulling cottons
Lynching minds way before the Klan got em'

Oceans filled with emotions of lost commitment to respect women's holy
entrance
Oceans filled with emotions of lost passions of men to smuggle their
manhood in other brothers asses
Because we feel comfortable being in the rear
The back of the bus
With junk in our trunks
Sucked and stuck in time zones when healing was

> **S**emen
> **E**xploded
> **X**-ing out
> **U**s and our
> **A**ppreciation for
> **L**ove

Black bruises on mahogany skin
Kings of the jungle releasing their loins
In a rush
To hide their crippling humility
They once were lions
Prideful and strong
Everything got flipped when those boats and chain came along

# Your Right as an American
## 3.21.07

It was once said
a patriot must be prepared to defend its country
against its own government
and treason will not prosper
and the declaration of impromptu rights
tells Americans to fight for DEMOCRACIES
however there are so many idiosyncrasies
that push me to question
WHAT IS THIS WAR FOR?
it couldn't be for the 80 Billion dollars a day revenue
that the government knew would come from bloodshed
it couldn't possibly be the spread of infectious democracy as a cover-up for
criminal activity
no, this war isn't about CIA smoke and mirrors or magical Weapons of
Mass Destruction
it was constructed in our legally binding Constitution that America would
become the LAND OF GREATNESS
and this war could not possibly be the thing to catapult that
tell this to the families who received folded flags and empty promises of
tarnished honors

tell this to the refugee camps and the children who learn their schoolwork
in bomb shelters and walk through war
America is so damn selfish
a brat who throws tantrums
imagine your picket white fence being drench with bloodshed
and your Mercedes S Class becoming a target for bombs
the constant stench of flesh . . . oh yeah . . . . . and 2.3 children and a puppy
to match
imagine famine and genocide, think about those golden arches of MickeyD's
changing into burning crosses
close your eyes and imagine your dream bride, being molested by your
colleagues, your brethren
your soldiers
now imagine you in the uniform, in the mist, with blood and dirt in your
sight, blowing up women and children, spreading disease and death
you are the soldier
. . . . imagine you pulling the trigger
now open your eyes, and breathe for a minute . . .
tell me, IS THIS WAR WORTH . . . your AMERICAN DREAM?

# All you see is a Nigger

You know, you happen to be the mastermind of ignorance
Your negativity is simply brilliant
I take your insults as compliments
Because the fact that you care so much about me makes me content
I cry not to please you but to choke you with my hazardous waters
I let you push me a little
So that I can soar farther
Yet all you see is a NIGGER
My round eyes hold all of the world's sincerities
My mind creates all of the earth's inquires
The beat of my heart moves the sun and the moon
My sighs bring the rain
And my smiles make the flowers bloom
But as I hang from a rope
And slowly my dignity chokes
You'll never knew I was humanity's mother
Because all you see is a NIGGER
If I called you chinks, mobster, crackers, or red-neck fools
Would I be considered a BIGOT, EVIL, or a RACIST too?

When I cry for REPERATIONS but know I won't receive a damn thing
When I REFUSE to pledge allegiance to the flag
But I'd rather 'Lift every voice and sing'
The fact that I am human, then to you didn't matter
When all you see is a NIGGER
In the 60's black was the thing to be
To be a nigger was a MOCKERY
But to me there's no "black land"
I want my FEET to touch AFRIKA'S SOIL again
When you threw my ANCESTORS into the Atlantic Ocean's salty water
All you saw was a NIGGER
Now THE WORD is used in a COMPASSIONATE way
Instead of the formal, THIS IS HOW we say 'hey'
In attempt to stop YOUR SKINS from burning in MY SUN
Integration of the RACES has begun
How can you PILLAR through my people's sweet stuff and
Suggest that slavery might be over
It couldn't be cause all you still see is a
NIGGER

# Spoken N' Heard contest

## *To Langston*

My name should be Spoken N' Heard
Because I shake the mode with the power of words
I wake niggas out of their slumber ignorance
And demand them to make a difference
It ain't rocket science
CHANGE GON' COME
As soon as men resist the urge 2 cum
And fight 2 eliminate guns
My nickname will be protest
Because I sat next 2
Revolution in a playpen
and even then I played with my pen
to twist words into pretzels of righteousness
and salt away all bullshit
I help women find their missed monthlies
By reminding them of the shine in their royalties
I coach them on knowing themselves as I know poetry
For I rename me spoken word exclusively
Speaking words of history
Where mothers birth nations
And define civilization
Yet women haven't been the same
Since their youth were ripped out of the womb
Rape cut their umbilical cord and forced them to consume
Life on their own
My tag is universal since I fly through time zones
CHANGE SOON BE HERE
And I will wipe all of the fear out of babies eyes
And fill in all the why's

As to why they are over weighted with burdens with DIABETES, AIDS,
and SEX
Because they seem to forget the universities resting next to the Nile
Where only European Cavemen were the wild
Music moved through palm trees
And Psalm 23
*"Ye though I walk"*
Bare footed on broken glass, barren streets
As teens become addicted to ecstasy and zombies to a new Jay Z beat
Instead of studying **Nastradamus**
To relieve the anguish of society
      Yeah I Spoke N' Heard
      Of dreams deferred
      Sitting on pissy wood next to crystal stairs
      As hatred stares force me to bare my deep anger
      For slave ship anchors
      That have made Afrika a stranger in the heart of this
      American Diaspora
These assimilated toddlers have forgotten their mother
And bling bling or BET just acts as a pacifier
In the desire
For us to stay blinded
    UNREST GONNA BEGIN
Cause my first name be SPOKEN N' HEARD
And the last is WORDS

# Chasing The High Stars

## 06.17.04

All my heroes were on heroin
I watched them raise their pipes in triumph
John Coltrane, I wonder what was in his veins
Huey P. Newton's face disappeared so fast
It made me forget the past
I saw Billie Holiday on a street corner
In Harlem chasing white dust
Selling black and blue ass
Whitney says crack is whack
But Bobby be bi-polar
So they buy more of that good stuff
My lady came home 'Singing the blues'
For her 'Mahogany' skin was too much of a sin
And crack highs was the new in
You just blazing beautiful
And too hot to touch
Stars from every coast
Boast about the thrills of the game
But most crack heads are the same
Covered in the beauty of rotten teeth and decaying spirits
Sagging skin, veins filled with sin

All my heroes were on heroin
Yes the greats had a hit or two
I watched them slide down in the ecstasy of intoxicants
From the bottle to the needle
Black eyes on Tina
Heavy metal across Jimi Hendrix's chest
I have watched them die and rest
Still wondering what was in Coltrane veins
What powder pimped Billie?
How many pills Dorothy Dandridge popped?
Was it Bobby or Whitney, who's high was on top?
Yes Huey begs for dollars in the subway
And Jimi only has six fingers to play
          his love serenade to cocaine
All of my heroes were on heroin
Never recognized it when I was young back then

# ♀ Mother ♀

Yesterday I sat down
and talked to Mother Earth
I was in awe,
The way she made
The breeze flow through her
                       Locked hair
Yes I was there
When rain fell from her eyes
As she looked at the AIDS population rise
No Lie
I heard the thunder
When she screamed
About murders, and homelessness, and destruction of the masses
She yelled "This is Blasted FUCKERY"
And I chimed in
We sipped herbal tea as her fingers twisted
The oceans currants
I sat there in amazement
As she took all of the beauty from children's eyes
And painted the sunset
I rested
In the bosom of her warmth
As she commanded the crickets and stars to
Lull me into a peaceful sleep
And in the morning
I awoke to her
Sun filled smile
Bright as eternity

# Begin

Righteousness seeps through the ink in my pen
And I do not know where to begin
I know I have to rewrite history
As far back as when they robbed our royalties
and told us his story instead of our story of our glory
Where queens' centers were rubies
And the stars were money
I have to erase the back lashes
That clashes with my grandfather's beautiful skin
But I don't know where to begin
Whether it be the Kentes in **Jufuree**
Or the young diamonds
Tarnishing their priceless for freedoms in the Island of Goree
Words of passion and revelations drop on my paper
Like slave ship anchors
In the deep blue conscious
Of my triangle existence
And I don't know whether to mention
A mother's child being slathered from her belly
Or kings becoming 'young bucks' reproducing with queens that aren't ready
So because of history's genetic ties we can't really blame R. Kelly
His dick wasn't really his since
He was under the master's whip
Of fresh whips, fat checks, cheap ass
And fans that flicker out of sight
Like project lights
And now we have movies like "The Original Sin"
But how do I begin
To describe the master minds
I mean master's mind
Behind the largest
Cultural Holocaust
That ever existed in any history
That will outlast history's impact

In fact
It was so powerful . . . that juice full skin
With MELANIN is just seen as BLACK
Well black out
All that textbook mumble
Because lies is the only thing it defends
And how can I begin
To talk about Reparations
And repeat bus strikes
Or fire blazing crosses at night
Or the three K's in America
That installs fear in the eyes that twinkle with greatness
And hold the key to all that life misses
Rhymes splash texture into the essence of my piece
Like how a piece can send someone into a peaceful sleep for eternity
Not to mention kill HUMANITY
Guns cripple the legs and communities of God's people in one clear shot
Sodom and Gomorrah suck the life out of marriage
And introduce little boys' ass to cocks
And now we have mad cows because of the way they are killed
They still remember how good it was when they relaxed and nigger hoed
the fields
'Getting hoes is my field' rappers proclaim
About a fast money game
With fast endings
And raw feelings
About "What is it all for?"
it really don't matter
if you cant breathe no more
my ink leaves marks on my paper like black eyes on mothers
but where do I begin?
I know I have to revise time
But I am running low on blue lines

# GODISNOWHERE

*God is Now Here? / God is No Where?*

Monotheistic boldly you keep asking me
HAVE YOU BEEN SAVED?
And I hang my head because I have been too busy
Watching premature babies being placed in their graves
No, I have not been dipped
For my soul still clings onto the culture that was whipped
Out of our bones, blood, and psyche
What can your "GOD" do for me?
HE IS THE EMACULENT, BRILLANT, SALVATION FOR THIS
NATION
HE PLACES THE SUN IN THE SKY AND THE SHINE IN
CHILDREN'S EYES
HE IS THE FATHER-
       Not my father!
My daddy is that crack head on the corner
Where is his honor . . .
For unpaid child support
And black eyes on my mother
HE IS THE HEAVENLY FATHER!
What is heaven?
Fifteen year old girls being gang-raped in an alley
Bullets in bodies daily
What is paradise?
       His promised milk and honey?
Why are there ghettoes, why are there billionaires, and then families
without money and a meal?
SISTER HAVE YOU EVER BEEN BLESSED?
No, I was too busy cleaning up poverty, crime, and the government's mess
SISTER, HAVE YOU NO FAITH?
IS THERE A SOUL IN THERE?
DON'T YOU KNOW . . .
           GOD IS NOW HERE!
sorry . . . but
           GOD IS NO WHERE!

# Free My Brother

Free
Mumia Abu-Jamal
No lethal injections for a cop he did not make fall
Fuck your legal system that is infested with cops who invest in
Stealing a free man's soul
And pumping thousands of bullets wrapped in iron around the ghetto
Yes free a revolutionary who moves with poetry seeping off of him
The panthers are becoming endangered
And as long as Jamal waits for death we are in danger
And as long as Charlton Heston dreams of bullet babies and has
NRA tatted on his chest
There will be no rest
Free my BROTHER
Or I will be forced to pick up each of the 41 bullets that were flung out at
Amadou
And shoot corruption from the sky
And from behind the oval office
Not even the best lawyer can prosecute my defense
For I am protected by truth and virtue and all the wondrous ancestors of
my past
If Jamal is not unshackled
Not one crooked official will last
As Bob Marley once said
"I feel like bombing the church, now that I know the Preacher is lying . . ."
No one else with melanin richness will be seen innocently dying
For a crime not committed
FREE MUMIA!
Before I flip
The suspect is not a black man this time
Cops and the media are the killers

'If it bleeds it leads'
blacks lead the headline
the American political system is the suspect this time
last time
the time before time
slavery time
once upon a time
before we were colored time
a time to kill time
Harlem Renaissance time
Prime time
KKK time
Yes Free Abu
Before I flip
He didn't kill that Philly cop in 81'
Yes, explain to me how
Five shots can be plunged into a cop's chest
From Jamal's hand
When he rested face down in the concrete
With a bullet in his chest
To call his own
I guess we should thank Samuel Colt for creating the revolver
Well the world revolves
And the destruction you shoot out
Will penetrate you later
Free Mumia Abu-Jamal
Before I lose my cool
It don't take law school
To notice the truth

# Stopped Looking To

It wasn't always a time when I wrote . . .
I remember vaguely I couldn't breathe right
Because my lungs were filled with glitz of open promises
And I couldn't find asylum in begin alone
It was a time when I smiled to be complimented
But my smiles no longer shine because of the rivers around it
A long time ago I wasn't conscience of my royalties
So I was prone to rape, and genetically worth nothing
I once forgot that between my limbs life formed
I stopped looking to

Live
And started just being
My heart was worn on my wrist and in my ears
Bling bling was the sound it made
I allowed misfortune to pass for some DVD's and a new pair of shoes
I didn't listen to my gut through my new headphones
I stopped looking to

Strive
And started doing
Doing what the average bitch did
Because when I looked in the mirror all I saw was permed hair and no crowns
I must have forgotten that my soul shined through my eyes
Cuz I am wearing hazel contacts now
I didn't know my blood was black gold
Since I always saw it wasted on street corners
I stopped looking to

Learn
And started trying to earn

Earn street credibility
Instead of spirituality
I knew nothing of the religion that was created to honor me
I thought pyramids were just sand and I was too far gone to see
Boys were becoming my high
They made me feel like how it felt when Isis dipped her toes in the Nile
I was too                    GONE
                                        I stopped looking to

Laugh
And started opening my legs
Sex was kryptonite
And I thought I was superwoman
I was the sole supporter of America leaving Iraq alone
Cuz I NEVER used a rubber
I was getting paid, begin laid, I was feeling justified and grown
        Me and DICK
I am straight
                                        I stopped looking to

Last
And started to change
I was the shit and could outlast time
But . . . then my period was late
I wasn't tripping though because
Bush supported abortions
AND weed
I didn't care about what could have become of my seed

*I could outlast time*
*Me and dick, I am straight*
*I STOPPED LOOKING TO*
*All I saw was permed hair and no crown*
*Crown . . . crown . . . crown*

"Miss . . . Miss your baby is crowning"
I was too far gone to murder my child
So now I am drowning
In sweat, tears, and afterbirth
16, a mother, and I don't even know what I am worth
but then I hold my sun up so I can see his pinkish face
                              and everything comes back to me
me and dick are no longer straight
my roots become kinky and twisted to hold up my crown
my king tickles my intellect as my feet rest in the Nile
the sun touches my skin and makes my black blood run
my womb blooms as it finds its purpose written on the pyramids walls
I STILL believe in America leaving Iraq alone
But rubbers are no problem at all
I started to breathe again in the light of my son's eyes
                                          I stopped looking to
Be
And started to live

# I Made my Own History

Is it better to speak or be spoken to?
screaming words of streaming semen
sliding down my thigh as I try my best to resurrect
men from within my womb
I did not write poems or starts protests
I processed my own form of revolutions
I gave and gave and gave and gave
to the common man, Black man, White man, Spanish man, Jewish man
no man was safe under my command
I fucked all men and I started my own revolution
bringing to the table a young face, thin waist and wet hole.
is it better to speak or be spoken to?
to talked or be talked about?
I have known gossip that slips off lips and runs down mouths as I pass
by . . . .
jealousy leaks from women's veins
as they refrain from asking me why I take their men away
but I don't take . . . I give and give and give and
I create revolutions of my own
therapeutic rocking between my limbs
condemns men to forget the ANGER that they feel
when they realizes just how real
the world gets without a job, no home, children to support, no resort, and
no assets

so they rely on my ass to get them by, to provide a high
with my young face, thin waist and wet hole
is it better to listen or be listened to?
I've heard the names I am called
hoe, slut, bitch, tramp and the list goes on
but how come no one has ever called me a martyr for the cause?
I've caused many revolutions to come about
see, in my world there is no way out
so I make the most hollow part of me a tunnel
so that others can travel on fallacies of passionate paradise
I gave and gave and gave and . . .
still my name is not in the history books
maintained my skills and perfected my looks
never got a chance to show the true me
I was struck and fucked and sucked and . . . you know the rest
placed in an unending cycle where I became the prodigal image of affection
I was desire and I was a warrior
laid down several times on my back to support the cause
laid down many men with my skills and I have resurrected
still . . .
is it better to speak or be spoken to
screaming words of streaming semen
sliding down my thigh as I try my best to resurrect
men from inside my womb

# New Redemption Song

♪ "Emancipate yourself from mental slavery. None but ourselves can free
our minds" ♪
That's what Bob once sang
But we can't emancipate if we won't allow our unity to ring
We bust guns into our brother's hearts
Since our shackled minds won't allow romance to creep into our bedrooms
after dark
I close my eyes and hum to myself
I see black men who prophesize on that bling bling wealth
I see black woman, who were the roots
Set aside their royalties and prostitute
I see black eyed peasy-head children
Who are indoctrinated into violence;
Bleach on their skins and contacts in their eyes
Sugar waters keeping them on an all day unnatural high
What happened to when street poets use to write "Dear Mama" letters and
harmonize "the sky is the limit"
DID WE FORGET?
What happened to when men were fathers and not baby daddies?
Why are women now bitches when we used to be the Eve behind every Adam?
WHERE ARE OUR ASSATA(S) AND MALCOLM(S)?
What happened to the street riots that used to shake up Birmingham?
Where are our drumbeats?
Why don't we scream and kill for the knowledge we seek?
Like Maya once said
"You may write me down in history, with your bitter, twisted lies. You may
trod me in the very dirt, But still like dust, I'll Rise."
This revolution is phenomenal, can't you hear?
Have no fear . . .
I am still that black supremacist here to let you know
Forget what ya heard, and you can take that to COINTELPRO
I am not here to flow about all the sweet love stuff
This jamboree is about getting fired up
I have a new redemption song
So.
♪ "Won't you help me sing, another song of freedom, cuz all I ever had
Redemption Song, Redemption Song" ♪

# Poetry Café

Smokey darkness illuminates a light of conscience that I almost can't handle
There is a beat here and there, a rhythm I know so well
It is my heart carried away by the melodies of music and words making sensual
The herbal incents tickle my sensitive smell
As my eyes water with every syllable
My little poetry café
Cups clinging and feet tapping in pure joy
My lips demand for everyone to look for a new reality
I sing and dance entertaining my soul
The tea in my hands keeps away the cold
Maya Angelou, my manager is in the back asking "What is this rhythmic revolution worth?"
Should we return to HIP HOP?
Do you remember when Kings of NEW YORK said things like "DON'T PUSH ME CUZ I AM CLOSE TO THE EGDE"
        Close to the edge of the stage
I am trying not to lose control
As smoky darkness illuminates a light of conscience that I almost can't handle
I clear my throat
                                (um um)
and start the show

# Next High

I can't stop shaking
    And digging in garbage cans ain't worth shit
And the drug dealer won't give me what I need by sucking his dick
      So I itch
      Bad
    For one more hit
I can't even smell me anymore because I am sitting in a puddle of piss
    In a dark alley
Waiting for an old church lady to walk by
    So I can get by
With her church money
      I NEED ANOTHER FUCKING HIT
And I can't take it anymore
I wipe snot from above my lip and picked up a brick
      This lady don't deserve to live
I have to get what I need

        BOOM
She's down on the concrete
And I got mines and hit the street
    With gleam of popping veins and highs all night in my head
    And there it was
    My lover
I wrapped a rubber band around my arm
Applying pressure
But then . . . I changed my mind
    I needed a high no one could measure
So I stuck a needle in my neck
Oh this- this feeling is better than sex
    This high makes me wet
I slide down in a puddle of piss
    Try to ride out this shit
I close my eyes
    And pray for my next high

# My first Performance

I stand on stage
Looking as if I am going drop some hot shit
But I just let one word drip from my lip
    R A P E
And all I hear are people gasping for air
Cuz one single word has touched their cores
      I see men squirm around anticipating another

          *I hate niggers cuz they ripped*
          *Through my essence and sucked the*
          *Fucking life out of me POEMS*

I also see the eyes of some women begging to tell
    How . . . .

          *It feels with your vagina laying*
          *Next to you in a criminal's hands*
          *That you don't know or love him*
          *And you place a pillow over your head*
          *Pop pills, and cut wrists so that*
          *You can't feel him type shit*

But I don't say another word
I just stand there openly pouring me
Into the teacups
That sit unattended by
The audience who
Is still tripping off one word

# My Mother Use to Sing 2, 3, 4, 2

## 05.31.04

My mother (2)
Used to dance (3)
With pole to call (4)
Her own (2)

Yes as I learned my alphabets
She toyed with sequins G-strings
And as I grew up she had this song she use to sing

*"Lord let my thighs stay tantalizing*
*let my behind be hypnotizing*
*so that*
*heat can rise*
*and the lights won't die"*

my mother (2)
used to dance (3)
with poles to call (4)
her own (2)

As I became rebellious
and tried to fight what was me
my mother mastered
seduction
and suction as she became greedier
we didn't need the benjamins anymore
our lights had life preservers

digital cable television and food in our kitchen
but mommy could not pee straight without leaning on a pole
she couldn't walk without her behind
swinging in a circular motion
and the "hands off rule" was now null and void
yes my mother
was doing another dance
singing another song
*"Thank God for my thighs*
*street corners are the life*
*my sixth grader is content*
*she don't need me as I work*
*the cement*
*thank God for your blessings: sex, drugs, money, and my pimp"*

my mother (2)
use to dance (3)
with poles to call (4)
her own (2)

I am now grown
And my hands are ruff and ashy
From fighting off the crack heads under my bed
I had different kinds of monsters
Like a different "uncle" every other week
And much experience with cocaine cutting
And black-eye-ology on my mother's face
Hoe is the word that rang out in my mind
24/7

724 was our apartment door
7: 42 in the morning was the time
my mother snuck in to my room to fake her responsibilities
she would stroke my head . . . at 8:15
then tell me she needed my bed
for "her company" at 8:20
yes my mother sang so beautifully
and I tried everything not to hear or sing like her
but I ended up on stage yelling out my own tones
to keep the house hot, the fridge full, and the men happy

*whispering*

my mother (2)
use to dance (3)
with poles to call (4)
her own (2)

*I spin (2)*
*And harmonize too (3)*
*Letting the music flow (4)*
*Like her (2)*

# Superman

Bright lights burn my pupils as I squint to perfect my image of you
I used to think you were Superman and that you had uplifting powers
running through
But the streets were your kryptonite
And I could not conquer you with the essence of me
But still my lights grow to purify what I see
They twinkle and illuminate
I now realize you are no longer my immortal hero
Magic powers and a cape can't hide what you feel
I tried to be down with your mission
But I guess you saw my fear with your x-ray vision
Superman you were so close
And that's the part that hurts the most
We shared fairytales of kids and me being your wife
      You were so close
But my grip missed as you jumped and ended your life

# Savannah Summer Nights

It is a power pull
face black and blue
hands mounted on the head board
back arched, thighs raw
teddy bears thrown on the floor
eyes closed praying salvation will burst through the door
with an automatic in one hand and a towel in the other
to bloodily murder him and clean away his sins
I was nine back then
knees in my chest
his nibbling on unformed breast
it is a tragedy
twelve years old and dealing with pregnancy
passing through times blind
never showing emotions
tears rolling down my eyes, waters choking
blood trickling down my thighs
on the bathroom tiles
gripping the tub trying to catch my breathe
then someone walks in a gun and a rag
she cleans me up and sends me home
I dressed up in black prepared to mourn
my best friend has gone
she murdered my rapist
and I haven't seen her since.

# A Full Night

Heat rest heavy in the room
and slowly reality of me being nothing but naïve
unchanging and perfect in my imperfections
no protection
from a man's fist
that pounds away at his own beat
we played
he laid
and I stayed for the game
yet as I skipped classes, I was being schooled
that I was not ready for a cruel unedited world
filled with
      cliff hangers and chin breakers
pronouns and twisted forearms
      as I was dragged down hill
and down flights of unpredicted kicks
      to the chest
*and I though I was blessed*
being able to use trickery on a man
taking his money
all the while gambling
      on whether my sun would continue to shine
low blows to the spine
is this what it feels like to be dying?
how shall I resurrect?
      how did this matter manifest?
all for a car ride here and there, dollars slipped, heaven laying on my breasts
how oh so quickly hell rose
as his anger grows
      into mainstream domesticated violence
I was silent
as I rode the train
one shoe gone
too bruised to go home
so I rode on
till first period came
and the cipher continued.

# God Bless the Child

Ebony eyes harbor tears of ebony aches
living life, gambling at all stakes
they said when it rains it pours
and thunderous trials fall on her shoulders
she is the one
who tells her story in a beauty salon
kicked out because her innocence was gone
had a child at fifteen and became a mother while she was still a preteen
juggled homelessness and unattach/ment to a mother who disowned her own
faced the world without a shield
God bless the child
she is the one
who I call a friend
forced to grow up quietly within
sinfully spinning webs of problems
impregnated on cold stairs
faced cold stares and no understanding
momma said she ain't having it
pun intended so she ended it
on the chopping block
at the chop shop
problems sucked up a tube

but she was still consumed with pain and hatred
praying that she could import death
because she was guilt-ridding with the life she was told to abort
God Bless the Child
she is the one
who looks in the mirror
blood shot eyes, tear stains on her cheeks
masquerades her pain as she poetically speaks
heart aches, she finds no self-beauty in her image
she is void and just manages
to survive living a life of lies
wondering what's in store feeling empty and lost
family pressure on her shoulders and she is forced
to be an overachiever
missing miss monthly, and family
remembering a lifetime of pain
bloodshed and it's sad
because God has blessed the child
who felt alone
who cried on her own
who survived through the storm
who inspired me to write this poem

# Little Black Boy's Poem

little black boy
be brought boys
starter boys
be block boys
slinging rock boys
them cock back boys
sell crack in capsules corner boys
grew up playing cops and robbers with gun toys
now must toy with the possibility
of his morality weighting more than his weight
he sees no other fate
so he willingly opens Pandora's gate

little black boy
with little black eyes
that hide behind fiery highs
holding pain inside
told to man-the-fuck-up
cuz real men never cry
now he lets bullets fly
through torsos, he's too cold
been closed up so long, now he's cut-throat
tatted tears on cheek bones
marking murders that his gun owns

little black boy
sitting in the back of the class
with top notch clothes
and no real goals
can't read to meet the standardized means
so he slick talk's his way through school

dropping out, he's a damn fool
finding pleasure in fast money and easy pussy
playing life like it's a guarantee
no one sheltered his mind and told him what he could be
so he fucks 'em all day and all night freely
slinging dick and caught a disease
laying pipe and spreading HIV
little black boy
with something to prove
baddest nigga in the hood, he stayed making moves
heart harder than project cement
caught a couple of cases and now his life is spent
grabbing his ankles in dark cells
never thought he would get fucked as he watched his drugs sell
had police watching his every step, they were always around
now he is serving double life in lock down

little black boy
oh what you could have been
could have changed the world
or cured cancer
you were the answer
but oh how sad it is to see
a little black boy living this life
with no way out, can't run from the strife
instead of being gangsta you could have been the sun
and if only someone had held you and loved and reared you well
and taught you and honored you and gave you a stable home
then I would have no reason to write
A LITTLE BLACK BOY'S POEM

# I've Got a Reason to be Ego-Trippin'

Biologically you cannot beat me
my kinky hairs are designed to uphold crowns
my broad back and thick thighs prevent me from going down
my black blood runs freely over centuries
creating babies and revolutions before sunsets
while you built sand castles, we built pyramids of intellect
racing around the world and made it back in time to harvest fruits of labor
across triangles of watery graves
having cornrows braided into our psyche
yet still biologically you cannot beat me
faster than a speeding bullet
you took a lot from us and we still succeeded
called us niggers, devils, and monkeys
sucked milk from our mother's breast and still cannot digest
that we are superior
called this world an equal opportunity
yet you had to create slavery
lynching and killing trying to control me
melanin drench, the longest time spent
we've cultivated long before you caught the drift
danced when you crawled
ruled when you roamed
survived where you couldn't
created what you didn't
Biologically you cannot beat me
history already told you that
your women created dresses to resemble the arch in my back
mentally raped and physically pillaged through my abundance of kings
just to feel the heaven I've always known down in between
you've washed in the Nile
shot down the Sphinx nose
captured and sold
and you still know
that if we went 200, 000 years more
whatever you tried to be
You still cannot beat me

# Ain't No Problem Being A Bird!

I heard Isis was a bird too
and I am sure she was flyy
had men flocking at her feet
supreme to all, she needs no validations
gold dripping on ebony skin
locked hair blowing violently in the wind
if homegirl were here today I know she'd be BAD
walking like she held universes between her thighs
spitting rhymes that flow like rivers, beaming sunlight from her eyes
dipping toes in the Nile as niggas try to holla'
but they can't come close to her earthily glow
trying their best to dip in and out, spitting their tightest flows
but she's heard it all before
I heard Isis was a bird
and I am sure she was flyy
rocking purple garments with gold trimmings
I could just picture her pictures on the inside of pyramids
she was no average chick
if homegirl were here today I know she'd be BAD
that round-the-way-chick that everyone wanted to kick it with
brains and beauty, I bet you Isis even had a big booty
I always heard Isis was a bird
and I guarantee she was too flyy

# On the Subway

*Ode to The Last Poets*

On my trip to the realization of my youthfulness
I get on a subway filled with intertwine flesh
I sat near a blue jacket juxtaposed with a pair of sluggish sagging jeans
I saw ears of bling bling and hands weighted down with rings
Splash of red, mixed with green, strips of white and dots of purple
Nikes and Jordans, ponytails
Hoodies, tight pants, and fingernails
I caught a glimpse of blonds, brunettes, and afros holding the rail
Can you find the underlining pain in my youthful brothers and sisters?
Will you be able to hear our burning determination flicker?
All forms of beauty joining up in my realization
As I write in the crowded train station
Kingston and Throop is my mecca
NEXT STOP, NEXT STOP
Off into the world I go

# Slavery

Let's take it back to
"A Nigger I am Not, A Nigger I will never be. I am Not Afraid of freedom
or prosperity."
I am not afraid to address in my hooks
SLAVERY
The greatest crime of malice destruction of a
Culture,
Native tongue,
Birth rights,
And humanity
SLAVERY
Jews riding with Jewels
While Niggers get stuck with no bucks
Jews were paid the price for Hitler
And Niggers are still comfortable being Nigger
Knowing Slavery was the greatest HOLOCAUST
SLAVERY
Black males becoming young bucks, being plucked out of the equations
Black women are AIDS ridden
Because brothers bend over in jail showers
To become weapons of mass destruction
Men on men infect, semen defects
And women let their bodies accept the erection
No protection
From a nigger with promise
So promiscuity is honored
No responsibility, no strings attached
Just a monopoly, no real money
Niggers getting caught thinking they are hard asses
But real gangsters don't sit behind bars

They own bonds, richer than stars
They build jails to destroy the masses
America's masterpiece is brothers congregated on the corner
Selling drugs thinking they are ballers
But they are just another figure
On a consumer chart
Bullets through our hearts
Bodies hanging off of CRACK rocks and CRYSTAL cliffs
People dying from cigarettes and marijuana spliffs
People getting shot for that bling bling scene
People killing for that mean green
Women looking more like men everyday
Willie Lynch has finally gotten his way
SLAVERY
Education crippling our minds
Graduate with MASTERS and still no jobs to find
Salaries getting lower and gas prices increases
Needing shelter, but rent is too steep
Angry mothers aborting unwanted blessings
Missing the reality of their actions
Fathers are no longer, we just have baby daddies
BET and UPN corrupt everything we see
Niggers throwing their cards in, their hands folded up
Enjoying the hells of Babylon
No one fighting for Mt. Zion
No one sees the need
And it saddens me
That in the year 2005
We are still in SLAVERY

# Even God Rested on The Seventh Day

voices of wisdom
sipping iced tea under palm trees
preaching prophecies, ashamed of the black community
saying "child wipe down your hands"
remove the blood and pamper your wounds
let down your guards, salvation will come soon
today let the wind play in your hair
let the sun pierce your eyes, sit back without a care
salvation will come soon
turn off your phone, let's communicate
set aside your picket signs, stop trying to pontificate
voices of wisdom
kissed my forehead
and feed me well
gave me a cool drink
to drown out the hell
that burned in my throat
I sat back and set my duties aside
put the keys down and enjoyed the ride
eyes closing, breath smooth and deep
forgetting the struggle for a minute and slipping into sleep

# Pocket

Do you have a pocket? Because I am looking for change
Are you willing to praise? Because I can't stand for you to complain
Could I have your ear? So you can witness my ingenuous figurative language
Anyone have a band-aid for my soul, because I've been hit with oppression's cut
Do you have detergent, because I am looking to gain
Standing above me shielding my roots from rain
Squeeze nature's juices right from my veins
Cut down my trees, and plant hatred white and plain
Do you have a picture, because I am searching for an image
You stole my dignity and royalties, they were never lent
My message shouldn't have been twisted, you knew exactly what I meant
So rally up your Klux Kluck and Mr. Klan
Because my tribes have new pockets, and we are gonna make some change

# Write Baby Write

How do you get black babies to write?
How can you show them education is the key to this fight
For limitless existence
In soaring past vacant lots
That remind them of vacant dream
That the ghetto don't cradle
How can you demand them to be hopeful
When the sky pours disadvantage constantly
And reminds them of their mental slavery
What do you do when their minds are content with project cement
And desires of unrealistic luxuries
That are not meant for one man to own
But then again Bill Gates can't relate
With a crack head for a cousin
And roaches that come out from under your pillow by the dozen
How do you get the youth to see
The metaphors in their eyes?
Such as the gleam of their pupils reminds me of the sky
And how will they learn to love Langston Hughes?
If they can't sit still from being abused
By sex and gun play in cartoons
And being forced to consume
Little Debby ass and 25 cents sugar waters
How do you push them to strive for the better?
How do you muster up the strength to say
"Believe Child" when thousands of things aren't going their way
How do you get black babies to write . . . ?
You start with me

# Your Glory Can't Shine Like Mine

I sit on my throne as a high goddess
My rubies shine and my eyes glow with God/dust
My enemies pointing spears at my back
but God told me to dust my shoulders off
I let one tear roll down my cheek because I feel sorry
For those who hold envy in their hearts
I rule over my flock with hands as soft as rose petals
But my voice is as strong as rare metal
I play no games
I hold no shame, I am a warrior priestess
I have the gold coast opened at the tip of my feet
I fought off colonial administrators in Abyssinia
I sat on Asante thrones in Ghana
I picked up fallen, stolen Africans in the Atlantic
I had Underground conversations in Mississippi
Burned selling blocks in New York
Drove above speed limit on the New Jersey turnpike just for sport
Nigger racing, nigger chasing
I row row rowed my boat out of Louisiana
I cried tears larger than Katrina
My black people drown with slave ship anchors at their ankles
And George Bush tried to angle his defense
For being absent when waters choked our humanity
And images flashed across television screens
Black blood flowed freely
And all CNN thought about was Kanye saying "George Bush don't care about me"
Or you, or us, or we
Bush was there for the tsunami
but when black folks parish it's just an average threat
But let me digress
While you digest
I will be sitting on my throne, still a goddess
Back arched and eyes shined with god/dust
God on my right telling me to dust my shoulders off

# The Cocky Artist/Sex on Stage

Softly I provoke thee
To mentally evoke me
Massage messages in your brain
Drop knowledge like tears of rain
Work you over and leave you with a feeling of twisted happiness
Braid-ing metaphoric ghetto melodies in ya psyche with erotic bliss
Letting the word 'son' slip forcefully off my lip
Don't trip
I call you son cause you shine like
Don't let your fear of my deep unknown
Stop you from dwelling
Because once you hear me work your ears with my rythmatic tongue
You will know I was a love daughter of Heru the eternal sun
So how can you ask me to teach you my shine?
You'll never pass the grades; your flow will never be as tight as mine
So sit back as I rip through your thoughts and zone through time
Don't worry about what I am doing up on this stage
THE MIC IS MINE!

# Never Knew Love Like This
## 05.26.04

There she is
A black butterfly
Too fly
So fly
Yeah that's right fly
Dipped in red
Seductively sitting unknown to the beauty that she is
Yes she sits with headphones pouring good love music into her ears
And her head succumbs to the beat and the smooth harmonization
And she becomes blinded by everything else
She is temptation
And too fly
Yes just plain hype
And she doesn't know it
As the wind plays peek-a-boo in her hair
And the sun shines off her lips just to tease
And the clouds sit in her eyes
Shielding her brains from intoxicants
She be black and lovely
But not the perm
Yes I see her with undeniable style
And grace sits at her feet waiting for a lesson on posture
For she walks like she knows diamonds rest on the tip of her toes
And between her thighs
But she doesn't recognize
That her silky skin and curves make others want to
wrap around

Stay around
Bow down
For she is just too damn bad
Black butterfly
Whose hands stay buttery soft and warm
To smooth over crusted burdens of others
You should see
Her back which is never bent
Because her head is too high
She is fly
So fly
That's right go ahead and fly
I see her not knowing that she is changing the world with her smile
Even if it's covered with braces
People can't brace that
That she is too black
Africa in Addias and a Old Navy Shirt
Yeah drums beat at the same rhythms of her feet
And she doesn't know that when she steps on stage
And procreates poetry and births truth
In five minutes or less
She is like a hit of crack
Yeah man too addictive
And she can't get enough of that rush
No one can hush
The lion's roar in between each of her syllables
Yet sadly she doesn't see her crown
When she is crying on her pillow
But she is still queen

Because when she steps on stage she
Parts oceans
Travels centuries and time zones
Defines what is unknown
But she don't know
That she is a black butterfly
Too fly
So fly
Yes beautiful flower, daddy's property
Child of Africa and the Caribbean from seas to the Serengeti
Yes Ayanna fly
For you are a black butterfly
Dipped in red and seductive
Purple and gold with royalty
A flower that blooms throughout seasons
Yes too fly
So go ahead and fly
Off my love

# Her Image

### *to Muncha*

I look at this brown skin girl
Who's tears are the same as mine
I see her pain and I know she can find
An escape in me because I reflect
        She
I never knew someone could
See what bounced around in my brain
      But she can
And I almost can't remain
      Sane
Because tears choke my desire to hide
And in five minutes I have confided
Things that no one but she can unlock
And I am not
Even mad that she knows
      For she
Reflect me
      And I
Image her

*This poem was written for a dear friend of mine. The storm always ends with a rainbow. Your cloudy days will soon shift into sunshine. You will be fine, I know you will and*
                         *I love you Steph.*

# Pillow Talk
## 05.08.04

I clench onto you every time my world spins out of control
And there is nothing on the face of this earth that knows what you know
*Yes I hear you*
I am scared that I will die of the pain that makes my heart heavy
The hurt that squeezes the juices from my smile and makes me angry
*You will live if it were up to me*
*I will protect you and never let anyone see*
*The tear stains that remains*
*Wet on my surface many days after*
*You've cried*
*I will cover your face and your heart*
*When you feel the need to hide*
*I will fill in the void where love is needed*
*The most*
*I will be your mother when she is too stressed from work*
*And my touches will never come as blows*
*They will nurture not hurt*
*My words will forever be kind*
*Because I want to build your self-esteem, not damage your mind*
*I will love you even if you stop loving me*
But, but this love cannot be true
How can I pour all of my aggressions and emotions into you
You are not real and I am not really speaking to you
*I am here*
*And you are you*
*When you are with me*
*There is no ugliness, weakness, or hatred*
*You are just pure beauty*
Stop it
Don't sweet talk me
I cannot take all of these compliments
Because I don't understand it
If you are here now

Where were you then?
*Then?*
Yes back when
I was a child laying funky under a man's short comings
You said nothing
Then
But now you rock me to sleep
And you silence my screams
You hold onto my dreams
But you said nothing then
*Then?*
Yes back when he asked me to open my mouth
And proceeded to rip my heart out
Through my throat
You said nothing when I was popping pills and
Writing death notes
But now you serenade me
When tears enable me to see
A brighter tomorrow
*I said nothing then*
*Because I was unable to be heard*
*Through sorrow*
*I remember as he laid on you, you laid on me*
*And as you wished for death in your sleep*
*I made sure you would see*
*The next day*
*I recall the way your body bled at my side*
*And I was there when you tried to hide*
*In the closet from him*
*I heard everything when you were contemplating on telling them*
*And I respected your judgment when you didn't*
*Yes I was there*
*As I am here*
So how come I didn't hear you back then
*Because your soul is asking you to listen right now*

# Alone

my thighs sit coolly
bruised and on a wooded floor
my insides burn and I feel raw
my hands ache from putting up a fight
I never had monsters under the bed at night
I had doorways filled with regret
pillows on the floor drench in neglect
unformed breast rise up and down as I try to catch my breath
fears slide down my chins and land in my lap
darkness makes noise all over the room and I
and consumed with thoughts
ugly disgusting thought
of his manhood beating down on me
with violent blows
fast or slow
I have come to know his rhymes
and his desire grew with time
I stood in the mirror and looked at my tightened legs
swollen bosom and plump belly
cradling responsibilities that I was not ready
to handle.
writing notes of sorrow and pain
I popped pills to forget how it felt
and I was unable to understand the hand I was dealt
I keep it a secret feeling alone and sinful
I told no one thinking I was to blame
I was twelve years old and I was ashamed
tears flowed and pain grew
I was alone
I was alone
alone

# Our Saddest story

We've traded southern death ropes
for ghetto veins filled with dope
Cracked souls, vessels at the tip of our toes
Genocide and everyone knows
      Drugs run our communities
      Drugs are the new chains of slavery
Motherless children wandering, forever searching for a high like their mother's breast
Smoking weed, sniffing crack till their noses bleed, dying like the rest
Birth defects, child neglect, killing our kind, separating the herd
Listen to the words
      Drugs run our communities
      Drugs are the new chains of slavery
Have we become so low, that all we can do is get high?
We are not on flight, we are forcing ourselves to die
No longer does Jim Crow have control
Now we blow PCP and Meth made of Crystal
Imprisoned in our own brains
Poison in our precious veins
      Drugs run our communities
      Drugs are the new chains of slavery
Drug money, the new blood money
Niggers thinking they are playing a monopoly
But they are only pawns in our destructive history
Re-writing our saddest story
      Drugs run our communities
      Drugs are the new chains of slavery
Re-writing our saddest story
Re-writing our saddest story
Ruining our communities
Putting us right back in slavery
Re-writing our saddest story

# kAtrinA

We no longer have to remember times where our ancestors hung on Slave
Ship anchors
we do not have to discuss Middle Passages while throwing words of
knowledge across coffee tables
we must see past black women kneeling
in front of slave masters
sucking up whitened corruption
like Black women in church aisles in pastel
with walls plastered with the whitest master
sucking in scriptures
Ironic isn't it?
Called us refugees and spread us across our OWN country
levees broke and we were returned to slave auction blocks
sleeping on Katrina relief cots
displaced and ignored
The big house watched as waters choked our humanity from our veins
called us insolvent and inhumane
Bush's momma said we should consider this disaster a blessing and be glad
it rained
on our parade
One year later and New Orleans still swelters with the heat of oppression
and pain
Afrikans lived without homes or any dignity to claim
we've been whitewashed and dragged out to dry
bamboozled and lied to
and our government still cannot figure out the issue!
We are fucking pissed that you can establish democracy in foreign lands
but neglect to give your own people a hand
fuck you mean, everything is alright
Babylon lies ahead in sight
Thunderstorms crashing on Super Domes
but certain citizens could not find relief in their own "home"
and you call this the land of the free and home of the brave
I just see a country that was called, but NEVER CAME!

# Ms. Cook's Sonnet

Afrika is like mother's milk to me
Its hills like breast beckoning me to rest
In the peacefulness of her curvaceous bosoms
Its rivers and its waves of sand
Smoothes the hair from my face when I need affection
And her sunset lets my intellect prance around in a field of freedom
For Afrika is like cornbread and syrup
Resting next to the lemonade and hot sauce
Her deepest valley and tropics lull me into a sleep beyond eternity
As I dream of being the Gold Coast and the tip of the sphinx's nose
You shot me down but still my power grows
For the fire in my eyes dances
Twirling, spinning, falling, and jumping around
Afrika's pyramids
Mother Afrika fits me as cozy as
A womb
And I curl up clenching on to her feeling
In the ultimate
Fetal position

For she is like the miracle of resurrections
and the pains of pushing watermelon through centuries
Afrika is choking me
With pressure of understanding
How can I lose her ?!?
She is too priceless
Yet four letters continue to rob her blinded
AIDS
Mother Afrika was my hope
But now where shall I run to
When the world pushes me down and scars my knees?
MOMMY DON'T LEAVE ME!
Out in the cold, destitute and alone
For I still taste you on the tip of my tongue
And the whip's lashes
Still don't outlast your butt whippings
When I've done wrong
Afrika you are the light to all that is left to see
And if there is no you, then there is no me

# And You Thought Slavery Was Through . . . Not True!

## *The Greatest Threat Revived*

Crooked politics "use the law to abuse the law"
Millions of Afrikans fall
Under the weight of America's injustices
They step on us like roaches, forbidding us to grow and live
But I know that I have to be brave
Their guilty conscience makes them afraid.
If we took up arms and took on evil and walked in the light of righteousness
We could change things as is.
Crime overflowing, weed blowing, girls hoeing, education slowing down
our brains, drugs in our veins, and enslavement still remains
Remember Assata?
Remember what jail taught her?
Jail is a profitable business, can't you see
Still "legally perpetuating slavery"
Re-read the Constitution
Because the 13th Amendment mentions
"Neither slavery nor involuntary servitude, **EXCEPT AS A PUNISHMENT FOR CRIME,** wherefore the party shall have been duly convicted, shall exist in the United States"
They'll do whatever it takes
To keep us as CATTLE!!!!!
    WE MUST RATTLE THE SYSTEM
Convict them of their sins
That have spanned over centuries
Remember our rich history
Where sistahs like Assata would be the highest royalty
I know you hear me
WAKE UP GODS, AND RECLAIM YOUR SHINE
SCREAM OUT YOUR NAMES, LET THEM KNOW "IT'S MINE"
WAKE UP GODS, RISE AND FIND
THE STRENGTH TO BEING
Whenever someone tells you slavery is through you tell them
NOT TRUE!

# I've Been Around the World

I visited China yesterday, and saw black planes and smoke
I sat with Nelson Mandela in the Cape of Hope
In England, I was the one in the back seat of Diana's car
In Jerusalem, I was rebirth from A'llat to Allah
I spoke of reparations and true colors with Tupac in L.A.
Took pictures of Egypt, and chat with Somalia in Mali
Bin Laden had me over for dinner
after I witnessed America bombing Afghanistan
I was the rifle Moses carried to the promised land
I bathed in the Nile as Noah swam by me
I sang with Vikings in Germany and cried with
enslaved Africans in Mississippi
From the North to the South pole I have stepped foot upon
Antigua, Peru, and then to France with Napoleon
I've been around the world
Just a simple little black girl
Has touched every inch of this Earth
Although some are skeptical and just don't believe
That I have been around the world
I just say hello, my name is Eve.

# Crack Back

not gone write a love poem
its not the time
not going dazzle with wittiness or rhyme
I got a high on
crack hit the black community
like hurricane Katrina
swirling and rapid, lucratively destroying our legacy
can't be queens and kings with poison in our veins
called us drug dealers but we are soul sellers
making deals under the table, trades with the Devil
wrapping lips around glass pipes
sucking destruction down their throats
chasing highs holding on to high hopes
this can't be life
can't be right
can't be what we're made for
feet shackled trapped on obstacles
we could have gone so far
still we gotta move on
          gotta stay strong
hugging blocks chasing feeling of warmth

shattered because many nights have been fatherless
caught on powdered paradises and cooked bliss
it's a paradox of cotton picking and crack slinging
its an irony like
black mothers knelling praying
while her son blasts chests open
clap hands!
Maya Angelou once screamed
now niggers clap hands passing on poverty
powder cocaine rains down on black skulls
PCP crystals make the concrete shine
and it's just fine
being drugged
being hugged by narcotics
we do not own planes or boats we are just puppets
thinking that corner boys get quick buck
but they are just getting fucked
playing the role of the noose
hanging our dignity in tiny capsules
can't write no poems of love . . . . with a high on

# Scattered and Confused

There is an iron wall in my face
And life pressing against my back
Yet I still feel the sunshine, resting on my face
      There is still poetry in me

It hasn't dried up yet

I want to ball up and roll out of everyone's existence
Be forgotten, and freed from remembrance
I want to rewind the cycle of life, and be reborn into something other than I
I want to be unnoticed and silenced
      My tears to become rainfall
And my smile to replace the shine of the stars

Alone and surrounded with doubt
      There are weights on my feet and I can't swim
Water becoming heavy and I try to float
      There is still poetry in me

It hasn't dried up yet

Pain shakes me awake in the early morning
      I clench my pillow for mutual support
Try not to be too loud, for my cries will be misunderstood
I want to be put on ice and numb
My pains to dissolve like air
And my screams to become music notes
      B flat
Sharpen to rip through peoples' ears
Hear me sing
Songs filled with memories
      And stories universal
Shaken and stirred
Scattered and confused

There still poetry in me
      It hasn't all been used

# The Life, The Dream

What boats do we float?
To bring crack to the cities
Look at history
We've been hoodwinked, bamboozled, and tricked to think
Gun play and AIDS filled sex is the life
Why are our heroes illiterate rappers
Who pimp purple haze and fake the game
How come no rapper ain't ever rode through my hood handing out books
All they do is boost up drugs in their hooks
Where are our gun factories?
Where is our blood money?
No REPARATIONS
Look at the story
We are being twisted
Shooting our brothers, becoming monopolized bitches
Is this the life?
IS THIS THE LIFE?
Is this the DREAM?
Can't be as miraculous as it seems
Crackheads scrawling the streets

Zombie teenagers with Pradas on their feet
Mother Earth throwing tidal waves left and right
Knocking empires out of her sight
She is tired of her land being abused
This planet is being used
Sit and be schooled
Is this the life?
Brooklyn benches, broke down fences
Heroin addicts pile up and it serves no consequences
To our conscience
Children cutting class
Throwing up gangs signs and selling ass
What happened to picket signs and outcries about the Middle Passage?
We would have more revolutionaries if these children would stay in their classes
Is this the life?
Is this our slice of the promised pie?
IS THIS SWEET?
Is this the DREAM?

# Civil Right Struggles to Hip Hop Moguls

Where has there been a divine separation between the rhythmic cries of freedom to the syncopated lyrics of Hip Hop?
What happened to fighting for sitting in the front of the struggle, why have we become comfortable with females naked behinds?
From "Let Free Ring' to the contemporary 'bling bling"
Where is our purpose?
There are still gun shots at the sun, however our history has become dimmed
Now we are more concerned about what we walk in
Instead of who has walked before us, who has been through boycotts and sit in's
where are our books that taught us history
why have we become so consumed with our looks?
what . . . Afrocentricity ain't enough?
Are we afraid to be seen snug and smart, is that why our pants drag up the dirt?
where have the freedom riders gone?
besides being displayed on a graphic tee shirt
how have we become divided and conquered
confused and again manipulated, we've once again become consumer slaves
all the revolutionaries seem to be buried in a grave
from black panthers and picket signs,

to knuck if you buck and pussy exploitation in rap lines
what is our present beliefs on richness ?
besides killing our brothers, and 'bagin bitches'
Twenty Four inch rims lift us from the ground that our ancestors
used to cry, sweat, bleed, and die on
                                "we shall overcome, someday"
we went from freedom dancing, to jails,
our freedom wasn't taken, we gave it away
salvation used to be in books and scriptures
not bullets, drugs, expensive cars and new sneakers
how can we bridge the gap?
will our new leaders ever really be able to grasp
that the word nigger means ignorant, hateful, and degrading
and it is what it is with or without a certain ending
whether it be an "er" or an "a", nigger is another way to keep us enslaved
it's a shame how quickly we've become rap warriors weak and played
we were once freedom soldiers strong and brave
Where have we been? where will we go?
From Civil Right Leaders to Hip Hop Moguls

# Untitled
## 06.19.04

Dear Lord the world is asleep
So now is the perfect time to talk
I am sorry I cannot hear
You through the pressures of life
But your word says you will always be by my side
So therefore I will take my mind off of
Failures, anger, miscommunication, missed monthlies,
yearly anguish, and dwelling wishes
I will be completely open
As I write under the light of the street lamp
I pray my intelligence
Will be enough to illuminate
       God it's five in the morning and I have nothing to do
So I will curl up at the corner of my bed and talk to you
Shall we discuss the wrong turns
This generation is making
Or what is really happiness?
Will we pontificate on the effects of sex in the media?
Or will we chill and listen to each other breathe?
Savior I can't sleep
And I am tired of being cradled
Tired of trying to play asleep
When I am fully awake
God . . . I am not sleeping
How about you?

# To them Niggas who be spitting Fake Hip Hop

I cannot be limited by paper
Back up before you taste my anger
For you cannot prophesize and this is not about what you feel
I ain't no fucking rhyme
I don't care about what chrome you spin on
Cuz you're spinning into an un-measurable hell
I don't care about how much your pockets swell or the weed you sell
Cuz you can't puff me out
     And yes
Spoken word has span across
Seas and landlocked niggers
Who refuse to soar over Babylon
I cannot be categorized by rap lyrics
This princess be priceless
Take your exploitation somewhere else
You have stolen the talents of griots
And added a bitch here and there
You don't deserve to speak
and I'll add a motherfucker so ya'll insignificant niggas can hear
Your bling bling has just burned out
Your shine can't go against the sun
       child
So ice up your ass as much as you feel like
But I will continue to throw
Salty sonnets into the nine gunshot wounds that you tote like it's progress
You ain't even worthy of my dollar, 50 Cent
Illiteracy ain't cute in 06'
So read a book
Or 2
Or 3
Let's see
"The Miseducation of You Negroes"
"Why the Caged bird is still in jail part 3"
"For Colored girls who think being video hoes is Enuff"
shall I continue . . . or is my beat up?

# Who Knew Hip Hop Would Take It This Far?

I heard a song on the radio today
      Couldn't catch the words, but I loved the flow
Couldn't relate to the messages, but America loves to know
      That every time my radio blows
Niggaz, Bitches and Hoes are at the forefront
Sipping vitamin water killing vital images of valued Afrikans
Knowing their words are used as weapons
Mass destruction in their intro         ductions
Collecting duckets of bling bling, slinging that mean green
Selling high hopes of getting rich by selling coke
      Destroying Black people with every stroke
Of their repulsive tongues
Blowing up big time, exploitation of innocent dreamers with guns and rap
rhymes
Bullet proof vest, hollow chest, female disrespect, ghettoes unrest
      Struggles that manifest
Because of GQ niggers with big check figures, shipping loads of lies into
the pipes and veins of my hood
             NAH HOMIE IT'S AIN'T ALL GOOD
And they blame the youth
      The Youth
         The YOUTH
For creating this monstrous deception of the truth
But the Youth I know get shot off project roofs

Banging bootlegged masquerades that rappers inject
    That rappers infest the media with
Little girls in stores shaking their "Laffy Taffy" behind closed doors
To little boys that *flip the china white*, smoking *purple haze*, living *bloody red days*, hiding from *them boys in blue*
                     Who knew . . . . Rappers would destroy Hip Hop
Who Knew?
    Rappers could rape queens in sixteen bars
Who Knew?
    Rappers would take it this far
Who Knew?
    Poetry was sodomized in disguise by iced out guys in rented homes, in rented cars, with rented hoes leaving holes in the ghetto
Who Knew?
    My niece would learn how to 'drop it like it's hot' before she could spell REVOLUTION
Who Knew?
    My nephew would live a life of confusions, *art vs. gunplay* before he even reached the third grade
Who Knew?
    The man I will one day marry likes 'booty poppin' on the handstand', thinks 'it's no fun if the homies can't get none' and drug dealers are the ultimate man
*I heard a song on the radio today . . . . If only you knew*

# A Brooklyn Bench

do you know what it is like to feel
someone else's blood run down your chin?
      you can't run.
your brain cannot even tell your feet to move
instead you shake involuntarily, uncontrollably
      on a Brooklyn bench
where you knew he sold drugs
but you told yourself nothing is thicker than blood
so you bring your cousin chicken and a Pepsi
disregarding the street life you despise
      and now you sit on that very bench
drenched, tasting his blood
hot and sticky summer day
murder never made the papers
niggas dying in the projects is a daily event
      so you sit still
hoping the next click is aimed at you
so that you don't have to see him lifeless daily in your mind
but the unmasked shooter turns and walks away
knowing that you know the game
and you will remain quiet
      and them unnamed
so you sit there with
brains on your shirt
      BOOM!!!
is all you hear
that's it
even as your family rushes to your side
and takes you inside
and cleans your outside
they cannot help you hide
from you biggest fear
      your dreams
BOOM!!!
how many of you sleep with this
whispering in your ears?

# Letters That Never Made It
## 09.18.06

*For Amadou 10.10.74-09.01.06*

I sit doubtful
with a drawer full of unsealed letters
cradling heartfelt messages never mentioned
and tearfully I tear through mounds of discomfort
as I wonder why?, how?, who?
no one answers
but my sorrowful whimpers
that fall systematically on top of crinkled papers
with penetrated ink and words that dance around
forming fragments into phrase to sentences, pauses and statements
that have been left untold
unheard by your wanting ears
that just need reassurance
but the letter never made it
they fell secondary to unnecessary holdups
and now I wait up for your phone calls
your warm ambiance to brighten my day
your sweet smile to let me know everything's okay
but I am just cold and numb
feeling like my right rib is gone
thinking I will never again see the sun
or be able to face your daughter and sons without
breaking down and fading out
and lumps of regret get caught in my throat

because I should have called, could have wrote
but then again that not the part that hurts
It hurts on Mondays when the wind blows roughly through the trees
and Tuesdays when the raindrops sprinkle across the cement
or Wednesdays where happy thoughts of weekends pleasures lie
even on Thursdays when the sun splashes across the sky
It hurts everyday every hour every minute every second
It even hurts in between those seconds that I can't count
There is no amount of words that can contest
my regret for not sending you
every letter of dreams, fears, inhibitions, wishes, and feelings
now these letters are taking up space
and suck up my soul
The man that once held me in hugs, I can only grasp through photos
I don't think anyone knows
exactly how it feels
to lose someone as special as you
every time I signed the bottom of a note
I should have felt grateful that I was able to write your name
no longer will I get to address another letter
Dear, Amadou.

# The End

I woke up and realized
The end is near in sight
And my passion rose as I clinched my weapon
And busted shots of poetry into the atmosphere
Yes . . . we soon be there
So polish your crown and collect your royalties
Let's keep riding Gods!

# Why YOU Were Made

### Cathie Wright-Lewis
### 5.22.04
*An extra treat*

I see your
Broken ankle chain,
Branding iron back stained
Rifle-Strap slapped across whippings' wounds
You maneuvering through
Projects and plantations screaming, *"Ya'll can come too!"*
Your wisely wheedled words make me more brave
You're Harriet returned
Moses of the 21st century runaway slave

With words like lightening striking across the sky
Spotlighting the pain we try to hide
Revealing concealing pressures of peers and years we've cried
Thunder clapping choruses harmonize with healing understanding
Sister you were born to change the wooden landings into crystal stairs
Without judgment, without fear, evacuating evil—without care
I just want to know where are you taking us
Harriet's seed
So I can provide whatever you need

Moses of the 21st century runaway slave
I bow as a witness to the future I crave

You are the light in the land of the blind
You were made to be heard.

# Special Thanks

To a God that strengthens my spirit, mind, and body.

To my Mother who is my best friend and my biggest supporter (Only God knows how much I love her). My father who is always there for me. My grandmother Meryl for being all the joy that I need in my life, she is my sunshine. To my Brother Amadou Abou Sette for being a prophet and a life saver GOD BLESS YOU: I MISS YOU SO MUCH, My brother Anthony, who introduced me to poetry, and to my other siblings Cathy and Alton, thanks for the love. To my nieces and nephews, I write to preserve the past and brighten your futures; I love you Manzel, Aminata, Christion, Anthony, Qiana, Chance, Shay, Madison, and Christopher. To my guardian ANGEL, my grandpa Otho O. Smith. To Marcus, you're the best babe!

To Ms. Wright-Lewis who put a pen in my hands when they were idle, thanks a lifetime. To Ms. Samuels who reminded me that I came from royalty, and who put Africa back in my heart. (Love and Respect to you Mother Africa.) To Ms. Cook-Persons the diva that brought my writing to the next level. To Ms. Maisha Fisher who is one of my inspirations (love you stay beautiful and live your life like its "GOLDEN"). Thank you to Masiira M. Abdul-Malik and Inskryber Editing for the WONDERFUL job editing and Nashaye for your beautiful artistic eye on the book cover! To Dennis Maurice, you inspire me brother! To my wonderful friends (girlfriends are like kisses, you can never have enough of them). To the ladies at Lincoln University who supported me, I love you! To Coota, Sharisse and Nyeesha I cherish our friendship!

To The Runaway Slaves of The 21st Century (Jelani, Jamar, Sadiquah, Sharisse, Nakita, Ms. Maisha, Ms. Cook, and Ms. Wright-Lewis,) you all have made me fall in love with poetry again every Tuesdays and Wednesdays. (You are my family, keep writing). Thank you to Ms. Terri Samuel my tenth grade English teacher. To Ms. Dawn Coleman, a Gemini that gave me a world of knowledge in just one year, thank you. To all of my family at Banneker . . . love you all!

To Xlibris Publishing, Lincoln University PA, To Ms Brenda Greene and Medgar Evers Community College in Brooklyn, NY, Polytechnic College Spoken Word Slam 2004, To PBS and BCAT television stations, To the Annual African Street Festival, To the National Black Writers Conference, The Nuyorican Poets Café, To Benjamin Banneker Academy for Community Development High School, to BROOKLYN NY! And to every stage and spot that I have been blessed to attend and perform.

To my heroes: the Last Poets, Amiri Baraka, Paul Lawrence Dunbar, Nikki Giovanni, Maya Angelou, Langston Hughes, Assata Shakur, Sistah Souljah, Queen Godis, Saul Williams, Jessica Care Moore, Gerren Liles, Willie Perdomo, Mumia Abu-Jamal, Amadou Diallo, Emmett Till, Abner Luima, Timothy Hansberry, Marvin Gaye, Bob Marley, the Roots, Jill Scott, Common, Erykah Badu, Lauryn Hill, Tupac Amaru Shakur, Christopher 'Biggie' Wallace, Def Poetry Jam, and to all those that have inspired me. To everyone who supports the arts. To everyone who made this book possible. Lastly, to those not mentioned, blame the mind and not the heart, love ya, PEACE.

CPSIA information can be obtained
at www.ICGtesting.com
Printed in the USA
FFHW020739080219
50477115-55701FF

9 781450 026185